Brothers Born a Month Apart:

A Surrogacy Story

Lisa Pontzious

Fulton Books, Inc.
Meadville, PA

Published by Fulton Books 2021

ISBN 978-1-63710-766-9 (paperback)
ISBN 978-1-63710-338-8 (hardcover)
ISBN 978-1-63710-337-1 (digital)

Printed in the United States of America

For my family:
My Dad for teaching me strength
My Mom for showing me love
My brother for the laughs
Thiru for being my rock
And Gavin and Logan for making all of our dreams come true

Mommy and Daddy loved each other very much, but something was missing. Mommy and Daddy decided that they wanted to have a baby. So they went to the doctor and made a bunch of special eggs.

"We have all these eggs. We are going
to make a baby!" Mommy said.

Mommy tried to carry an egg many times, but it wasn't working. The doctors and nurses tried to figure out the problem, but they couldn't.

Mommy and Daddy were very sad.

Mommy and Daddy had an idea and asked the doctor, "What if we put one of our special eggs in another tummy, do you think it would grow?"

The doctor said, "Yes!"
So that's what they did.

8

A few months later, the doctor put a special
egg into a nice, helpful lady's tummy.
Mommy and Daddy were so excited!

9

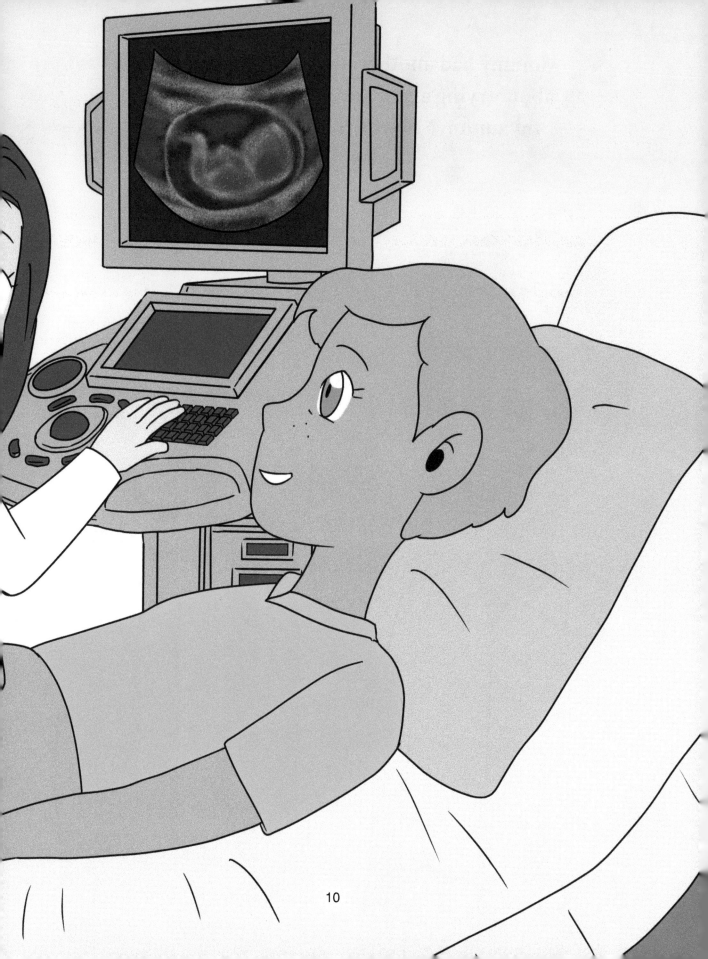

Mommy had another idea, "What do you think about trying again and putting another egg in my tummy? Maybe this time, it will grow!"

The doctor and Daddy thought that was a great idea!
Daddy told Mommy, "You are so strong!"
The doctor said, "She is determined to be a mommy."

Mommy and Daddy
went back to the
doctor. The doctor
put a special egg in
Mommy's tummy,
and they waited to
see if it would grow.

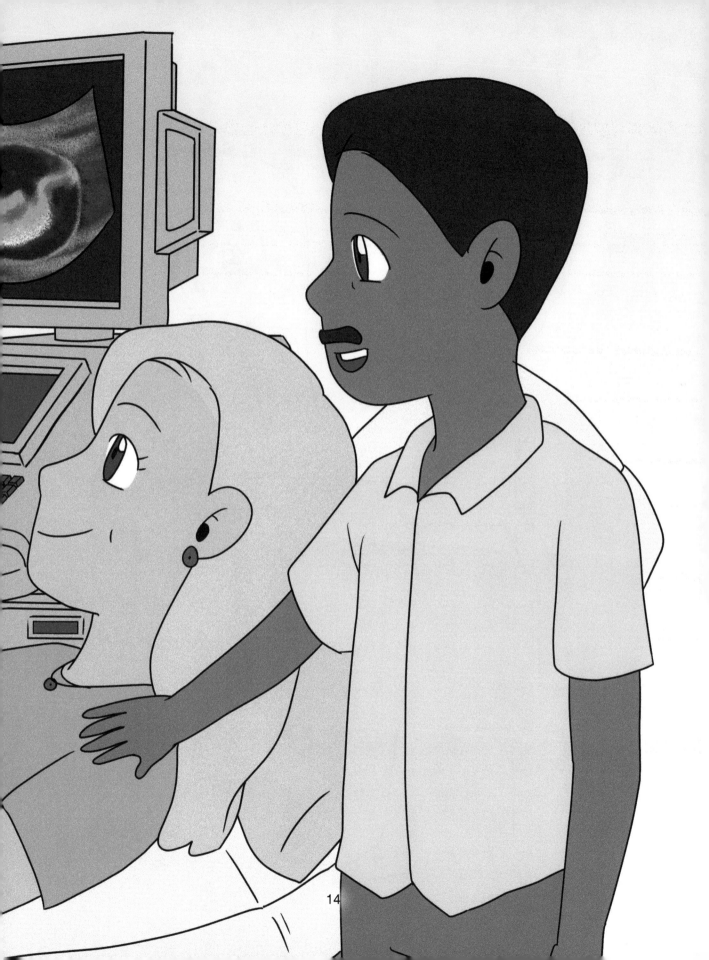

14

They waited and waited, and the two tummies got big and round. Mommy was very excited; she couldn't believe she was going to have two babies!

When it was time, the first baby came out of the nice lady's tummy. Mommy and Daddy named that baby Gavin.

Gavin was so special, and Mommy and Daddy fell in love with him right away. Mommy loved to hug and kiss Gavin and couldn't believe she finally had a baby. She was so thankful that the nice lady helped her to keep her special egg safe and help it grow into her beautiful baby.

Mommy would hold baby Gavin, and he would rest his head on Mommy's tummy. Mommy told Gavin that he was going to be a brother. Gavin smiled. Mommy couldn't help but smile too. She was so happy.

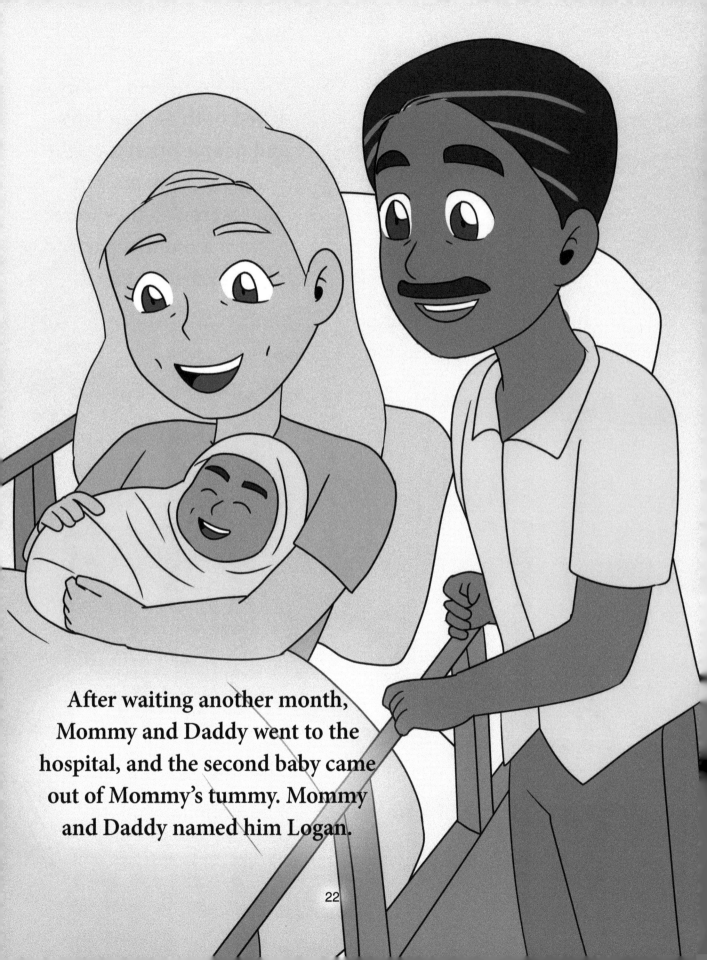

After waiting another month, Mommy and Daddy went to the hospital, and the second baby came out of Mommy's tummy. Mommy and Daddy named him Logan.

Mommy and Daddy loved both of their boys, and people often thought they were twins, but they weren't—they were born a month apart. They are brothers!

Gavin and Logan made Mommy and Daddy so happy, and their hearts were so full.

"I love our boys," Mommy would say to Daddy.

"I love them too," Daddy would reply.

Gavin and Logan were best friends from the day they were born. They loved to play with cars and dinosaurs and loved to be chased by Mommy and Daddy.

Sitting with the boys, Mommy said, "We are all so lucky and thankful for the nice lady who helped us make our family."

"Super lucky!" Gavin and Logan said at the same time, then they all laughed.

ABOUT THE AUTHOR

Lisa is a mother, a word that she was unsure would ever be associated with her being. After suffering eight miscarriages, countless shots, disappointments, and heartaches, Lisa and her fiancé turned to a gestational carrier to help carry their child. But Lisa and her never-give-up attitude decided to try again and to carry a child alongside her surrogate. Adding another shot to her already-rigorous regime, Lisa preserved. She is now the proud mother of her two beautiful sons who were born a month apart.

CPSIA information can be obtained
at www.ICGtesting.com
Printed in the USA
BVHW090308250821
615139BV00014BA/1134